D0734273

More Language
That Needs Watching

By Theodore M. Bernstein

WATCH YOUR LANGUAGE (1958)

HEADLINES AND DEADLINES (with Robert E. Garst; Columbia University Press, 1935, 1961)

More Language That Needs Watching

*Second aid for writers and
editors, emanating from
the News Room of
The New York Times*

by Theodore M. Bernstein

MANHASSET, NEW YORK

Copyright © 1962 by Theodore M. Bernstein

First printing

All rights in this book are reserved. No part of this book may be used or reproduced in any form whatsoever without written permission from the publisher, except in the case of brief quotations embodied in critical articles and reviews. For information address Channel Press, Inc., 400 Community Drive, Manhasset, New York.

Library of Congress Catalog Card Number: 62-18182

Printed in the United States of America

To the hundreds of captive

contributors without whom

this book would not have

been possible—men and women

who, day in and day out, strive

steadfastly and with no small

success to give the world a

good newspaper.

Introduction

Meet Junior. Readers of "Watch Your Language" will find no difficulty in detecting a family resemblance between that book and this offspring. Both descend in a direct line from *Winners & Sinners,* a carping collection of the magnifique and the miserable that goes out to the staff of The New York Times from time to time and is designed to raise their hackles and their performance simultaneously.

Winners & Sinners, an informal bulletin of second-guessing, was started in 1951 and has now accumulated almost three times as many outside-the-office, over-the-shoulder peerers as staff readers. "Watch Your Language" was a compilation of material that appeared in the bulletin between 1951 and early 1958. But time and The Times do not stand still. Many triumphs of reporting, writing, editing and headlining have appeared since 1958 and, alas, so have many slips, slubs and slurs. "More Language That Needs Watching" collects the more interesting of the new items for the enlightenment and perhaps the entertainment of those who are devoted to clear, concise and generally good writing and to the art of communicating the news.

The sinners, it will be found, greatly outnumber the winners. This should not be surprising, because, as was stated in the opening issue of *W & S,* "to do things properly is normal and even a slight deviation to the bad side is noticeable, whereas a deviation to the good side has to be quite pronounced before it appears to be anything more than normal." Nevertheless, it should not be inferred that newspapers, much less The New York Times, are the center of the solecism.*

If more solecisms come to public attention in the columns of newspapers than elsewhere, it may well be because more words come to public attention in the form of newspaper articles than in any other form. It may also be because the pressures of time, of distractions and of interruptions in newspapering open more possibilities for error than are opened in the more leisurely forms of communication. The newspaperman sometimes wonders if the public is really aware of this fact.

In a nebulous sort of way the public knows that newspapers are published in one hell of a hurry. But this nebulous impression comes chiefly from movie and television offerings. And what is the picture presented in those offerings? Scoop Smith (in real life his name more probably would be Arnold Dittenhouse) covers the big story, sometimes even taking a few notes. He bursts into the news room and orders the city editor to "hold the front page" (he

* A check of five dictionaries after this was written disclosed that all favor the pronunciation soll-ecism, and only one even allows the pronunciation sohl-ecism. But, honestly now, would you have passed up the pun on such flimsy grounds?

always knows instinctively that he has the day's lead story). He shucks his jacket, but never his hat. He twists a sheet of copy paper into his typewriter and, never referring to those notes he took, he starts rattling out the story. You see it crawling from his typewriter: "When is District Attorney Sam Shwabisher going to forget politics long enough to go after the real murderer of Pauline Hamilton? When are the corrupt police going to clap the handcuffs on Butch Glonsky? How long will it take. . . ." By this time the city editor, eyes aglow, is looking at Scoop's clattering typewriter. "Great stuff!" he exclaims. "I'll write the head for it." (The implication is that Scoop doesn't need to stop to perform that chore himself.) The next thing you know (without any intervening processes except the snatching of the copy by the blond, toothy copy boy), we are looking over the shoulder of a pressman at a crisp copy of the "Extra," while in the background the papers are cascading off the press. There in big type stretched across eight columns of the front page is the head the city editor wrote: "HAMILTON MURDER STILL UNSOLVED!" (The newspaper that would print that eight-column head is the one that would proclaim, "PRESIDENT McKINLEY STILL DEAD!") Scoop gets a Pulitzer Prize and marries the girl ("SCOOP SMITH WEDS CHILDHOOD SWEETHEART!"). Swelling music. "The End."

If a newspaper were really put out that way, it would have few readers, plenty of libel suits and certainly no Pulitzer Prizes. About the only things true to life in that picture are the typewriter, the presses and the speed. The produc-

tion of a real newspaper involves a great deal more organization, much more work, much greater care and, above all,
editing—the forgotten ingredient in virtually all dramatiza-
tions.

Let's get down to earth and see what really happens.

It is mid-afternoon and the office of the morning newspaper is quiet except for the typewriters of a few rewrite
men tapping out short stories of routine events. The man
covering police headquarters phones the city desk to report
a rather large theft of uncut diamonds from a dealer's
office—"Looks like a pretty fair story." Should he cover it
or does the city desk want to assign another reporter to the
story? He is instructed to remain on his beat. Arnold Dittenhouse draws the assignment. He is told the nature of the
story and goes to work.

From the headquarters man Arnold picks up the basic
facts by phone. A diamond merchant, Gregory Lee, has
reported the loss of $100,000 worth of uncut stones from the
safe in his office at 1661 Sixth Avenue. Lee says the stones
were there the previous afternoon but were gone this morning. The police have questioned everyone in the office except
a clerk ("Haven't got his name, but the precinct cops can
give it to you"). The clerk has not been questioned because
he left on a two-week vacation last night and no one seems
to know where he is.

Arnold next travels to the precinct station house and
buttonholes a detective on the case. He learns that the clerk

is Julius Feinguy, 22 years old, who rooms with a family named Fickett in Queens Village. He also discovers that the F.B.I. is investigating because of a suspicion that the diamonds may have been transported across state lines. Do the police suspect anything phony about the case—a staged theft to collect insurance or anything like that? No, they do not. Was the safe jimmied open or blown open? No, there were no signs that it had been tampered with in any way. Then it looks like an inside job, doesn't it? The police are offering no theory about it just yet.

A visit to Lee's office seems to be in order so that Arnold can at least get some idea of the physical layout. At the Sixth Avenue address the reporter is fortunate enough to find Lee in his office. He thus is able, in addition, to gather a few details about the personal appearance of the distraught, bespectacled, round little man who has suddenly found himself a figure in the news. Arnold is curious about how the safe was opened. Lee suggests the possibility that he may have left it open and unwatched very briefly the previous afternoon when he stepped into another room to answer a phone call. He has nothing else to add to what Arnold already knows.

At this point the reporter phones the city desk to report how the story shapes up and to see whether the office has any further information that would require outside checking before he returns. Time is getting shorter now, and he is told to come in.

Back at his desk, Arnold knows there are still one or two angles to be explored. There is also one piece of routine that he senses he must still perform, but for the life of him he can't recall what it is. He phones the F.B.I. press officer, but, as he expected, learns nothing except that the investigators would like to question Feinguy. No, they cannot say where they are looking for him.

Next he searches through the phone book for the Ficketts. (What is that piece of routine he has overlooked?) Mrs. Fickett tells him what she knows about her roomer, Feinguy, which is not much. No, she doesn't know his home town or where he went on vacation.

Ah, yes, that piece of routine. Send to the newspaper morgue to see if there are any clippings on Feinguy. Not very hopeful, but you never can tell. While he is waiting, he organizes his notes. At last the copy boy hands him the slim folder from the morgue. It contains a single small clipping: A five-year-old dispatch from St. Louis relates that Julius Feinguy, 17, won a city-wide essay contest. St. Louis? An angle, perhaps.

It is getting late, but Arnold now has a couple of more phone calls to make. First he checks back to headquarters. Are the police looking for Feinguy in St. Louis? The police won't say. Arnold drags out a St. Louis phone book. There's a chance. Feinguy is an unusual name. He finds a number and puts through a call. Yes, this is Julius Feinguy's mother. No, Julius hasn't been there. No one else has phoned, but a detective did visit her to ask the same question. What is it all about? Thanks, Mrs. Feinguy.

Arnold decides to let his paper's resident correspondent approach the St. Louis police and puts in a call for him.

Meanwhile, he has a story and probably an exclusive angle. It is time to begin writing. He checks with the city desk to inform the editors about the story and to get instructions about how much to write. He returns to his desk, feeds some paper into his typewriter and begins. He must hurry, he knows. The deadline is an hour and a half away. But it will take him perhaps an hour to write the story. And it has been drummed into him that every story that is to appear in the paper cannot go to the composition room at the deadline, because if that happened the paper would never be printed. So he writes as rapidly as he can, sending the story to the desk in short sections, or "takes." He pauses only to consult his notes and to take a call from the St. Louis correspondent. Out rolls the story, take after take.

What has happened up to this point is the exercise of the creative faculty of newspapering. The city desk and the reporter combine to bring the story into being. The reporter, now working at top speed, is almost completely preoccupied with his subject matter. Many fine points of writing, of presentation, even of accuracy may escape him. But he is backstopped. The critical faculty is now brought into play on the copy desk. His story is passed to a copy editor. Except for the news editor and his assistants, who oversee in a general way everything that goes into the newspaper but obviously cannot read closely all the thousands and thousands of words, the copy editor exercises final responsibility.

Let's call him Harold Aufseher. The diamond story is now

in his hands. He has been told by the city desk how long the story is to be. As a practiced editor, Hal knows that Arnold probably will exceed his limit (most reporters understandably do that) and so he is on the alert to trim out the soft spots as he proceeds. In addition he will try to tighten the wording wherever he can to save precious space. When the reporter writes, "one of the employes," Hal will condense it to "an employe"; when the reporter writes that the police "rushed to the scene," Hal will strike out the phrase as an unnecessary and self-evident detail. In the second paragraph he discovers an involved fifty-word sentence; he breaks it into two short, clear sentences. When he reads that "the tray with its little bags and boxes of stones were missing from the safe," he almost automatically corrects the grammatical error. He sends the lead to the composing room and picks up the next take.

Here he finds that Arnold has inadvertently begun to refer to Gregory Lee as "Mr. Gregory." Rather than interrupt the reporter he checks in the phone book to make sure of the man's name. However, when he notes that there has been no elaboration of the statement in the lead about "$100,000 worth of uncut diamonds, ranging up to nine carets in weight," he decides he will have to interrupt the reporter. "Who made the evaluation—the dealer, the police, the insurance company?" He returns to his desk and inserts the necessary information.

Next he deletes a quotation from Mr. Lee: "I always thought there was something a little shady about Feinguy." Libelous. He also deletes a quotation from Mrs. Fickett: "He was careless personally—fingernails always dirty and that sort of thing." Poor taste and irrelevant.

Smoothly and swiftly, his critical faculties always on the alert, Hal makes his way through the story. As he goes, he writes subheads in the copy—those little headings of bold-face type that are inserted to break up long stretches of gray type. And as he goes, he is trying to resolve in his mind what the headline should say. When the story is finished, he tackles the head. His job here is to condense the main news of Arnold's 600-word story into half a dozen words.

Arnold has been writing under pressure; Hal has been editing under pressure. Each has a multitude of things to keep in mind. The story, as it presently appears in the paper, is as accurate as they can make it; it is a smooth, lucid job of narrative and exposition, and it may even have some literary quality. Both have worked hard, if hastily, to make it a finished piece of news writing. For Hal, incidentally, it is only one of a dozen or more stories he has processed before deadline. He has had to switch his attention rapidly from robbery to rocketry, from budgets to bullets, from grand slams to great slums, from racket busters to filibusters. Is it extraordinary, then, that something has eluded him, that he has allowed a mistake to slip into print? It is perhaps not excusable, but it is at least understandable.

Winners & Sinners has been lying in wait. It may commend Arnold for an "inviting lead"; it may single out Hal's headline for inclusion among "trophies of a head-hunter."

But it may also publish an item something like this:

Mind your p's and carrots.'"$100,000 worth of uncut dia-
monds, ranging up to nine carets in weight" (Nov. 17).
Those things come in three varieties: There are carrots
that you eat to make your eyes blue, there are carats
that are units of weight of precious stones and there are
carets that are marks used by editors and proofreaders,
and sometimes we could use a lot of the third variety.

The purpose behind such an item is by no means to hu-
miliate the writer or the editor (a sinner is never identified by
name) or to pounce upon an isolated and unusual error. The
purpose is rather to call to general notice a mistake that might
recur and to try, by so doing, to forestall the recurrence.

It is not at all surprising, then, that there is a steady supply
of material for *W & S*. Newspapermen normally are not
heedless, but they are human. The hope is that a watchdog
like *W & S* will by its very existence constantly diminish
the stock of the stuff it feeds on. There is no possibility,
however, that it will starve.

The struggle of the free press to unearth the news and
tell it to the citizenry is challenging and continuous—and
fairly well known. The struggle to tell the news accurately,
lucidly and in flawless language is equally challenging and
equally continuous, but it is hardly known at all. Day in
and day out dedicated writers and editors devote themselves
to this struggle, and achieve an astonishing measure of vic-
tory. The public knows only their defeats; their triumphs go
untrumpeted.

T. M. B.

New York City,
September, 1962

More Language
That Needs Watching

ACCIDENTAL PUNS. A story about a tremendous increase in the consumption of fish carried the head, "Fish Scale Heights." If that pun was intentional, it was misguided, not only because it was a poor one but also because the straightaway story did not call for that kind of head. If it was inadvertent, it was equally undesirable, for just about the same reasons.

-w&s-

"First the tiger and an emotionally stable horse were encouraged to become friends. . . ." Equine-imity? Watch out for combinations like "stable horse." And for this sort of accidental pun, which appeared in a review: "At every dinner table someone has just encountered a French general—generally retired. . . ."

ACRONYM. "Mutual of New York has put a new man into its advertising and promotion department. His job is to tell why the insurance company spells MONY without an 'e.' In 1951 the company began use of the contrac-

19

tion. . . ." It's not exactly a contraction; it is exactly an acronym, a word made up of the initial letters of the words in a title or term, or of a combination of beginnings of the words. For example, "UNESCO" (*U*nited *N*ations *E*ducational, *S*cientific and *C*ultural *O*rganization) or "radar" (*ra*dio *d*etecting *a*nd *r*anging).

-w&s-

While we're on the subject—the apparent stranger at a cocktail party who slaps you on the back with a jovial "Where've you been all these years, you old son-of-a-gun?" is a disconcerting chap. You should know him, you think, but you can't place him for the life of you. Strangers like these sometimes grin at readers out of stories. Here is an example. The story said that a supplement to the weekly newsletter of the Committee on Political Education had criticized Richard Nixon. The seventh paragraph of the story began, "COPE said Mr. Nixon's proposals. . . ." COPE? That name would send any reader groping back up the preceding six paragraphs to try to identify the stranger. If you are going to use an unfamiliar abbreviation or acronym, introduce it properly immediately after the title to which it refers.

ADVANCE. "There was no advance warning, although an official had visited the dam earlier." As in the phrase "advance planning," the idea of "advance" is implicit in the noun.

ADVERSE. "He is an early riser; one of his first chores is to read the morning newspapers (and he is not adverse to reading about himself)." "Adverse" means opposed, antagonistic, hostile. "Averse," which is the word desired here, means disinclined, reluctant, loath.

AGREEMENT IN NUMBER. Disagreement in number between subject and verb is the most persistently recurrent error in news writing—and perhaps in other writing as well. Examples, with corrections in parentheses: "Dr. Trussell indicated later that the new school would probably be built in the Bronx, since that borough's need for new facilities were (was) so acute." "He estimated that one out of ten high-stake games were (was) played with a marked deck." "The navy announced that a task force, including an aircraft carrier, a cruiser and transports loaded with marines, were (was) steaming southward."

These errors do not, of course, arise out of ignorance; they arise out of haste and carelessness, out of failure to look back to see what the actual subject of the verb is. They are bad enough when committed by the writer, but they are unpardonable when passed by the copy editor. *See also* "one of the," "one or more," "what."

-w&s-

Let's face it: There are some nouns that do not comfortably accommodate themselves to the plural form. Here are some examples: "Steel and Auto Output Are

High," "American and Soviet prestige are at stake in the negotiations." Therefore, the only courses open are to take evasive tactics in a headline—"Output of Steel and Autos High," omitting the verb; or, in the story, to add extra words—"The prestige of America and that of the Soviet are at stake"—avoiding the necessity for the plural noun.

On the other hand, you should not mechanically decide that because the nominal subject is singular the verb must be singular. For example: "A variety of water, shore and marsh birds is attracting large numbers of nature lovers to the Jamaica Bay Wildlife Refuge." The important question is: To what are you directing the reader's attention— the idea of "variety" or the idea of "birds"? Clearly in this instance it is birds, and "a variety of" is virtually equivalent to "many." Hence, the verb should be "are." "Variety" could be the dominant idea—and the verb singular—if the sentence were of this type: "The variety of shore birds at Jamaica shows that food of many kinds is available."

To go on: "The prisoners were told to keep their yard clean." Fine, the prisoners share a single yard: "The prisoners were told to keep their nose clean." Pfui; the prisoners have more than one nose. Sounds elementary, doesn't it? But look: "The deadline is midnight tonight. Those who register after that must also provide proof that their car is insured." "Extra help for residents who have trouble with their state income tax is now being provided

at the New York District Office." Obviously in the first
sentence it must be "cars are" and in the second sentence
it must be "taxes" (unless it said "*the* state income tax").
A noun of this kind applying to more than one person can
be singular if it represents a quality or thing possessed in
common or if it is an abstraction or if it is a figurative
word. Not one of the three ifs applies here, however.

ALGER, HORATIO. "The chairman and director-general
of the biggest banking chain in the Middle East today
was once an unschooled door-to-door salesman in the
United States. This modern Horatio Alger of the Arab
world. . . ." Look, children, in your parents' and grand-
parents' day there was an author who created rags-to-
riches heroes. His heroes weren't named Horatio Alger;
that was the author's name. See, kids? Now you wouldn't
want Alger to go the way of Frankenstein, would you,
pets?

ALIBI. *See* "loaded words."

AMID, AMONG. "Among" means in the midst of count-
able things. When the things are not separable the word is
"amid" or "amidst." Therefore this sentence is incorrect:
"Masked firemen groped among the wreckage hours
later." "Wreckage" is a mass noun that does not denote
enumerable items. This sentence is likewise incorrect:
"Among the recent news emanating from Paris was a pro-

vocative item predicting the return of the stocking seam." The item was not found in the midst of one new, a second new and a third new.

ANENT. "Retort to Democrats Anent U-2 Cites Statements by President." Except in legal usage, "anent" is archaic and semiprecious. Why not "about"?

ARBITRATOR. A copy editor wrote a headline saying that "Arbitration Ends Air Strike Threat," then added a bank that said, "Kennedy Picks Mediators in Pan American-Pilot Issue." Mediators and arbitrators are not the same thing. Learned counsel informs *Winners & Sinners* that arbitrators have no power—and, in fact, no right— to mediate. Mediators act as go-betweens and try to work out an agreement, but lack any authority of ultimate decision. Arbitrators, acting as judges, hear evidence and make an award. The case is dismissed—with prejudice.

ARCHITECTS. "Architect is Skidmore, Owings & Merrill." "The architect is Voorhees Walker Smith Smith & Haines of New York." Although it is true, as the ampersands show, that these are firm names, the concerns are partnerships of licensed individuals. Surely it would make for more graceful reading to say, "The architects are. . . ."

ARDORS. "Khrushchev is Resting. Takes Day Off From Ardors of Hungarian Visit." Here is a rare situation in which we can observe the process of back formation—the coining of a nonexistent word from an actual word that is erroneously supposed to be derived from it. The actual word is "arduous," and the writer wrongly presumed it to be derived from "ardor," which is nonexistent in the presumed meaning. There is not the slightest connection between the two words.

ART TERMS. Care is needed in using the technical words of the art field. For example, the *Winners & Sinners* curator advises that "abstract," when used as an art term, is a verb or an adjective but never a noun. This is improper: "Three abstracts by Louis Rosenthal were exhibited. . . ." Make it "abstractions."

ARTHRITIS. "A new diagnostic procedure for arthritis of the joints was reported yesterday." Arthritis is always "of the joints."

AS FAR AS. *See* "so far as."

AS TO. In a phrase like "the question as to whether," the words "as to" are forget 'em words—that is, useless. However, this does not mean that "as to" can be eliminated invariably when it precedes "whether." Take this example: "Señor Nuñez was questioned whether Cuba intended to establish diplomatic relations with East Germany." It might seem that "questioned" is here exactly synonymous with "asked." That is not true, however, as becomes evident if the sentence is turned into the active voice. Whereas you would write, "Newsmen asked him whether . . . ," you would not write, "Newsmen questioned him whether. . . ." "As to" or "about" or "concerning" is necessary before "whether." English is sometimes a complicated language.

AS WELL AS. "He, as well as the producer, Jack H. Silverman, are Broadway newcomers." "As well as" is a subordinating, not a coordinating, conjunction. It is not the equivalent of "and" and its meaning (though not its grammatical function) is more like "besides." Therefore, its presence does not make the subject plural. The sentence should read, ". . . is a Broadway newcomer." *See also* "agreement in number," "plus."

AUTOMATION. The substitution of a man-driven vacuum street-sweeping machine for a man with a broom does not justify a phrase such as, "Street Sweepers Face Automation." Automation refers to the automatic control of an operation or process, especially by electronic means.

BEAUTY. "The beauty of such stations is that a pilot can pick up the signal beamed on any one of the 360 compass headings and use it to navigate." "Beauty" has to do with the senses or esthetic appreciation. As used here, it is purely colloquial, just one step above "the beauty part."

BELIEVE. *See* "feel."

BESIDE(S). "Beside Governor Harriman, Mr. Hogan and Mr. Crotty, the candidates chosen by the convention were. . . ." "Beside" means at the side of. "Besides"—the word wanted here—means in addition to.

BLOTTER. "Mr. Mangum was under investigation for removing from a police blotter the arrest of Mrs. Hazel Sharper." Two ledgers are kept by the desk lieutenant in a police precinct: the blotter and the arrest record. The blotter is a kind of log, containing sundry police intelligence but no notations of arrests; these are entered in the arrest record. Therefore Mr. Mangum could not have removed the arrest from the "blotter."

BOLT. The reporter wrote: "Mr. Saal is serving as a member of the Democratic county committee, a post he won by bucking the organization." The copy editor, deciding (correctly) that "bucking" was colloquial and should be replaced, substituted (incorrectly) "bolting." And here is something curious: Our political experts agree that the correct definition of this American term "bolt" is the one that appears in a British dictionary—the Oxford—which says it means to break away from a political organization, whereas an incomplete definition appears in an American dictionary—Webster's II*—which says it means merely to refuse to support. So our editor was right by Webster, but wrong, by Jiminy.

BOTH. The word means, in effect, the two together, and it is sometimes used redundantly when the two-together idea is elsewhere in the sentence, as: "The two are good friends. Both worked together at the New York Stock Exchange." Make it, "They worked together."

BRIGHT PASSAGES. Normally you would not expect the reporter who is rattling his typewriter in a race against clockhands that are circling relentlessly toward deadline to come up with writing of literary quality. Yet it is astonishing how often it happens. Fresh figures of speech, flashes of uncontrived fun, illuminating observation of significant detail and sometimes merely the melody of well-chosen words—these adorn many stories in any day's newspaper. You may be sure that such bright passages are not accidental. But neither are they laboriously fabricated. They spring from an almost instinctive way with words that is one of the marks of a good writer. The selected passages that follow, with the authors identified, may not be immortal lines, but they are at least remark-

* Webster's II, in *W&S* shorthand, signifies *Webster's New International Dictionary,* Second Edition; Webster's III signifies *Webster's Third New International Dictionary;* Fowler signifies *Modern English Usage* by H. W. Fowler; and Evans signifies *A Dictionary of Contemporary American Usage* by Bergen and Cornelia Evans.

able demonstrations of what it is possible for a pro to produce under sometimes intolerable pressure.

Most of the capitals of newly independent African countries have the look of a convalescent, of a large man who fell ill and no longer fills his clothes. (*Henry Tanner*)

-*w&s*-

Mrs. Charles Guggenheimer, chairman of Stadium Concerts, had a word or two to contribute. "I tell you they're all children," she said over the phone, throwing up her hands. Minnie Guggenheimer is the only person who can throw up her hands over the telephone. (*Harold Schonberg*)

-*w&s*-

Many of the sterling athletes are so wearied that they hardly have the strength left to do their television commercials. (*Arthur Daley*)

-*w&s*-

But every car became so overwhelming, so powerful, so chrome-bedecked that they all began to look alike and the goose that laid the golden eggs was cooked. (*Robert Alden*)

-*w&s*-

Just before the third race Moreno was notified that the stewards had made him a pedestrian instead of an equestrian for ten days, effective today. (*William Conklin*)

-*w&s*-

I am referring to the cricket match, written obviously in a way to convulse every last reader on the sceptered isle—and as wearying in its way, no doubt, as a long chapter on a baseball game would be if the vice were versaed. (*Charles Poore*)

-w&s-

In abstract expressionism, he thinks, the isms have "reached the apex of a retinal approach" to art—which means that the eye is offered "an esthetic delectation that depends entirely on the sensitivity of the retina with hardly any auxiliary associations." (This might be translated into middlebrow as "good to look at, but doesn't say much," or into lowbrow as "beautiful but dumb.") (*John Canaday*)

BULLET. "The 15-year-old boys are accused of having stolen 3,000 rounds of small-caliber bullets." "Young Buchanan told the police that he had wounded himself when he hit a bullet with a rock." Let it be noted, first, that a "round" is a unit of ammunition (therefore it would be better to say, "3,000 rounds of small-caliber ammunition") and, second, that a bullet is merely the projectile inside the cartridge (therefore the boys stole cartridges, not bullets, and Buchanan could not have wounded himself by hitting merely a bullet because there is nothing explosive about a bullet).

BURGLARIZED. "L. I. Home Burglarized." Colloquial.

CALIBER. "The policemen used their 38-caliber Police Specials. . . ." The resident gunsel points out that it should be ".38-caliber," the figure referring to the diameter of the bullet, which in this case was thirty-eight one-hundredths of an inch. He also notes that there is no such thing as a "Police Special."

CAREEN, CAREER. "A Russian-made jeep loaded with members of a Chinese Communist aid mission careened into a United States Embassy automobile." Conceivably this could be a correct use of "careen," but let it be noted for those who may be hazy on the point that "careen" means tilt or heel over, whereas "career" means move at high speed.

CEMENT-MIXER. A headline, caption and story all spoke of a "cement-mixer truck" that fell into an excavation. Our construction superintendent advises that there is no such thing. Cement comes already mixed. It's combined with water, sand, gravel and stuff to make concrete, and that's what the truck was mixing.

CIRCLE. "Thousands had circled around the bier." Strike out "around."

CITE. "Mr. Rogers cited that the amendment had been in effect only a little more than seven years." "Cite" is followed by a noun, but not by a noun clause. You can cite the amendment, but you cannot cite that the amendment, etc. *See also* "quotations" *and* "quoted."

CLIMAX. "The drop in popularity of the larger engine reached its climax last September when market penetration of the 'eights' fell to a three-year low of 47 per cent." "Climax," which comes from a Greek word meaning ladder, refers to an ascending series. But even if it is extended to mean the culmination of such a series, the direction is still upward. A low point cannot be a climax.

CO-ED. "Co-ed Commutes to Night Club." The caption referred to a Smith College girl and therefore was wrong. A co-ed, so the standard and slang dictionaries all tell us, is a female student in a coeducational institution, which Smith is not.

COLLECT. "Prince Charles, decked out in black riding hat, sweater and jodhpurs, collected a pony from the paddock and practiced in a far corner of the field." "Collect" means to bring together; you cannot collect a single thing. And the only animal you could collect would be a chicken in parts.*

COMMERCIAL NAMES. The problem of when to use commercial names in the news columns is a ticklish one.

* Whoa: You can also "collect" a horse, but that means bring it in hand and under control.

The adage—and if there isn't such an adage there should be one—"Why give it away if you can sell it?" is still valid. But it is not especially helpful since it so often must yield to the reader's rightful claim to information. A comprehensive code on when to use commercial names probably cannot be framed. But some suggestions can be offered, and will be herewith.

Use commerical names:

1. *If they provide necessary information.* A story said that diethyltoluamide was found by the Department of Agriculture to be an effective insect repellent. Without the name of a brand that contained this chemical, the story was worthless.

2. *If they provide pertinent information.* This kind of information would be akin to the name, age and address of the culprit in a hold-up story. It would embrace the name of the store in which an elevator fell, the name and channel of a TV program on which the Soviet Ambassador was interviewed and the name of the company sponsoring a golf tournament. It would include the make of plane that crashed (planes have varying sizes, capacities and power plants), though not usually the makes of trains, buses or automobiles that have crashed since the differences here are not generally significant.

3. *If to omit them is bound to arouse curiosity.* When you say that the TV commercials for one product have not been changed for years, the reader is curious to know which one you have in mind.

4. *If to omit them seems niggardly.* When you say that the dog in the picture is a greyhound "identified with a bus line," the reader knows which line you mean and it seems small of you to suppress something so obvious.

On the other hand, brand names should not be lugged in when they are neither pertinent nor necessary. Thus, there is no point in saying that the picture was "Scotch-taped to the wall" or that the sailors drank coffee, "either the regular or the Sanka variety." "Taped" or "stuck" would do in the first instance and "decaffeinated" in the second.

What all this adds up to, if indeed it adds up to anything, is to be solicitous of the reader's interests and to use good old common sense.

COMMON. See "mutual."

COMMON DENOMINATOR. *See* "mathematical expressions."

COMPARATIVES. *See* "other," "superlatives."

COMPENDIUM. "The new compendium of his many critical essays. . . ." A compendium is not all-inclusive, it is an abridgment; it is not the whole works, it is a précis; it is not big, it is little.

CONCLAVE. "Secret Conclave Winds Up World Affairs Discussion." A conclave (based on the Latin "clavis," meaning key) originally referred to a room that could be locked, and now means a secret or private meeting. "Secret conclave" is redundant.

CONNIVE. "In Jersey City, Donald Dawson, one of the President's aides, connived with local police to knock down the street barricades at one point along a Presidential parade route so that the crowd would overflow in a simulated mob scene." Strictly speaking (and what's wrong with that?), "connive" means to wink at or shut one's eyes to some irregularity. Therefore whatever conniving was done was done by the police, not by Dawson, who instigated the irregularity. What was meant here was "secretly arranged with" or perhaps "conspired with."

CONSERVATION. "Senators Receive a 22-Billion Plan for Conservation." The story was about a proposal by the Reclamation Bureau (and that should have been the clue) for developing water resources in the Western states. To put it simply, conservation is preserving what you have; reclamation is getting back what you have lost. The water proposal was designed to reclaim land for productive use.

CONSIST. "He added that 'conservatism at its best must be progressive.' This consists, he explained, of carefully weighing the cost of progress before rushing ahead with it." It should be "consists in." "Consists of" is used to introduce the component parts, as in, "Most of the Indian-Chinese discussions have consisted of private conversations between Premier Chou and Prime Minister Nehru." "Consist in" is used to define or set forth an identity. This was the purpose in the passage cited.

CONVINCE. "Three unidentified persons who had taken the girl to the airport tried futilely to convince her to take her seat on the plane." "Persuade" would be the proper word in this construction. "Convince" may be followed by an "of" phrase or a "that" clause, but not by a "to" infinitive. "Persuade," on the other hand, may be followed by any of them. The reason for the nonuse of an infinitive after "convince" may be merely, as Roy H. Copperud says in *Editor & Publisher,* that it "flouts idiom." But perhaps the reason for the idiom itself lies in the meanings of "convince" and "persuade." "Convince" has the meaning of satisfy beyond doubt by argument or evidence appealing to the reason. "Persuade" has the meaning of inducing or winning over by argument or entreaty appealing to the reason and feeling. In the case of "convince" there is a static situation, which does not in itself suggest a consequent action. In the case of "persuade" a shifting is brought about from one position to another, often with the implication of action to come— and hence another verb form, which may be an infinitive. But whether this excursion into the dark origins of idiom makes sense or no, the fact remains: no infinitive after "convince."

COUNCILOR, COUNSELOR. "Charles Muller, councilor of the Belgian Embassy, said the demonstration had been expected." In the diplomatic service it's "counselor."

CRITICAL. *See* "grave."

CURB. "He said he saw the inspectors curb a car on Roose-velt Road and remove three men from the vehicle at pistol point." The "Curb Your Dog" signs around town are part of the present-day ad-diction and are supposed to be bright; they do not pretend to be giving a serious new meaning to "curb." The use of "curb" to mean force or draw to the curb has no validity.

DAIS. *See* "podium."

DEAD BODIES. "They said that many dead bodies, mostly of children, were seen floating on the water." Strike out "dead." "Bodies" in this sense means corpses. You wouldn't speak of "live bodies," would you?

DECIMATE. A reviewer wrote, "A nuclear war someone started has caused fall-out that has completely decimated the entire northern hemisphere." "Decimate" means, literally, to take a tenth part of and, by extension, to destroy a considerable part of. The word "completely" betrays that what the writer meant was "annihilated," and with this word, by the way, "completely" would be redundant.

DESERTS. "The players showed an inconsiderate boy friend getting his just desserts." It's "deserts"—from the same root as "deserve." Deserts are what one deserves, good or bad.

DETECTIVE. *See* "plainclothes man."

DIPLOMAT. "The United States expelled two Cuban diplomats today. The Cubans, both consular officials. . . ." A diplomat is one who is engaged in or skilled in the conduct of international intercourse, and the term usually covers ambassadors, ministers, nuncios and chargés d'affaires. Consular officials, however, are of a lower order, often merely businessmen, and are not customarily classed as diplomats. *See also* "councilor, counselor."

DISAPPEARED. "The ship suddenly capsized and disappeared from sight." Delete "from sight."

DISCOMFIT, DISCOMFITURE. "To discomfit" does not mean to discomfort; it means to defeat, overthrow, rout. This is a misuse: "Mr. Shevchenko, a straight-talking farm expert, outlined his findings, many of them obviously discomfiting to the Bulgarian leaders. . . ." Another misuse: "For the Communist rulers of Kerala State, this morning's development was pure balm. It spared them the discomfiture of an immediate parliamentary debate." "Discomfiture" does not mean discomfort either; it is a much stronger word. If you suffer discomfiture you most certainly suffer discomfort, too, but the reverse is not necessarily (or even usually) true.

DIVERT. "The ship diverted from its course Saturday to pick up the captain of the French freighter *Thesée*." "Divert" is a transitive verb only. Say "veered" or "was diverted."

DIVIDE. *See* "separate."

DOCK. "A fire that began on abandoned coal docks. . . ." "Soon all four docks were ablaze. . . ." A dock cannot burn because it is the patch of water enclosed by piers or wharves. Only in inexact colloquial usage does dock mean pier.

DOUBLE DUTY. This is the sweatshop practice of forcing one word to do the work of two. It sometimes occurs when the writer is displeased by the word he ends his sentence with. For example: "Most cities figure on a 10-cent 'drop' for whatever fraction of a mile the meter is set." Notice how that little word "for" is manfully trying to serve as a preposition governing the whole clause and as a preposition governing "fraction"? It needs another "for" after "set," and never mind the anti-preposition-at-enders.

DOUBLE GENITIVE. A correspondent asks whether this possessive form is justified: "He also said that he had often been a guest of Mr. Goldfine's." The answer is yes; the double genitive seems to be a hoary idiom in English. Sometimes it even affects the meaning. For instance, "a picture of Mr. Goldfine" means one thing; "a picture of Mr. Goldfine's" means something else. Prof. R. W. Pence of De Pauw University notes that there is also such a thing as a triple genitive: "He is a friend of yours"; the "your" is one genitive, the added "s" is a second and the "of" phrase is the third. Maybe you can't buy much with it at the corner delicatessen, but it's an interesting item if you're interested in that sort of thing.

EACH OTHER. "President Eisenhower and Soviet Premier Nikita S. Khrushchev, who this fall will visit each other's country. . . ." "Each other" is regarded as a reciprocal pronoun, plural in its meaning; in the genitive it is equivalent to "their." Therefore it should be "each other's countries." Of course, in a different construction you would say, "Each will visit the other's country," but that, to repeat unashamedly, is a different construction.

EKE. "After a series of fits and starts yesterday the stock market eked out a gain." "Eke" has Anglo-Saxon roots meaning increase or add. When you eke something out you add to it or supplement it. What is eked out is not the thing that results but the original stock or supply. In short, "eke out" does not mean "squeeze out," as the quoted sentence suggests.

ELLIPSIS. "Following two days of cricket at Downing Stadium . . . it is apparent why cricket has not and will not make the grade." Ellipsis permits the omission of a word in part of a sentence if it can be supplied, or "understood," from a neighboring part of the sentence. However, after "has not" you cannot supply "make," hence the grammar is improper.

-w&s-

Another example: "Four of the six votes would be necessary for removing one or both the judges from office." You can say "both the judges," but you cannot say "one the judges." Therefore write, "one or both of the judges." *See also* "quotations."

ELOPE. The story said that "Mrs. Dorothy Wrigley Rich, 33 years old, and Thomas W. Chauncey, 45, eloped to Albuquerque," but only obliquely suggested that a wedding followed. It should be remembered that "elope" means only to run off, with the intention of being married; it does not include the act of marriage itself.

EMISSARY. "The Provisional Government has apparently received favorable indications from the emissary by telephone." An emissary is not only a secret agent, but also usually one who is engaged in something underhanded. The word commonly has a pejorative meaning. *See also* "diplomat."

END RESULT. "The end result of segregation and lack of compulsory education for Africans. . . ." An end result is conceivable in the working out of a mathematical problem in which there are intermediate results, but in good old everyday English an end result is simply a result. *See also* "mathematical expressions."

ENGINEER. The word "engineer" tends to be used loosely in the news columns, as engineer-readers point out from time to time. Example: "An engineer employed by a plumbing concern accused of submitting rigged bids to the Board of Education was arrested." Engineering is a licensed profession. It is doubtful whether the plumbing concern employe was a licensed engineer and probable that he was a technician.

EQUALLY AS. "The Indians are equally as fanatical in their hatred of the white Europeans who have led the

Katangese Army." "Equally as" is tautological. Vote for one.

ESCAPE. "Two prisoners were foiled last night in their movie-script plan to escape the Tombs." "Escape," as an intransitive verb, means to break free, and is followed by "from" or "out of." As a transitive verb, not followed by a preposition, it means to avoid, evade or elude ("he escaped punishment"). The sentence quoted requires a preposition.

ESPOUSE. "Former President Eisenhower suggested inferentially tonight that the Republican party espouse an overhaul of the nation's economic laws." "Espouse" is a kind of Sunday word like "vouchsafe."

EVACUATE. "Evacuate" can mean quit a military position and it can also mean remove troops from such a position. But notice in this odd sentence how it is made to serve both purposes simultaneously: "After Morocco won her independence, the King demanded 'total and unconditional' evacuation of the United States bases as well as French and Spanish troops." *See also* "double duty."

EVERYBODY. "And so everybody took their guitars and songs, their poetry and perambulators, their high-bouncers and dogs, and went peacefully home." Here is an instance in which the proper pronouns—"his" or "his or

FACILITY. Want to know what a "facility" is? In eight different stories it was: an auto inspection station, a home for the aged, a radio station, a hospital garden, a radar antenna, a parking garage, an industrial city and a rocket-launching pad. By dictionary definition a facility is something that promotes ease of operation. It fits scarcely any of the items listed. Indeed, one suspects that the word itself is a reporter's facility.

FAMED, FAMOUS. "Paul Engle, famed Iowa poet, was on the way to his summer home near here last evening. . . ." Why "famed" rather than "famous"? "Famed" is the participle of the verb "fame." Who famed him? The word is not incorrect, but rather suggests an attempt to avoid the customary one. A more important question is this: Why use such a word at all? If the man is famous, everyone knows it and you don't need to say so; if he is not, then the word is an exaggeration.

FEEL. "Feel" is not precisely interchangeable with "think" or "believe," although there is a tendency to use it as a replacement for both those words. Aside from its tactile meaning, "feel" means believe emotionally rather than intellectually, hold an opinion on vague or unexamined grounds: "The boy's mother *feels* he will recover but the doctors *think* otherwise." In the following example, since a thinking process—a count of votes—seems to be involved, "believed" or "thought" would be better than

Wife Learning to Drive, Husband Calls All Cars. (*Irving Horowitz*)

-*w&s*-

Phone Company Drops elsea From Chelsea. (*Harold Gal*)

-*w&s*-

Tipsy Passengers Won't Fly "High." (*Socrates K. Butsikares*)

-*w&s*-

Thurber "O" Stry Planned fr Stage. Blmgarden and Greene Will Prduce Musical. (*Jerry Gold and Joseph Michalak*)

-*w&s*-

Cigar Smokers Breathe Untaxed Sigh of Relief. (*Sam Haines*)

-*w&s*-

Kennedy's Chair Rocks Nation. (*Charles Friedman*)

-*w&s*-

Feathers Stir No Fuss. London Dealers Indifferent to Sale of Rare Plumage. (*Emerson Chapin*)

-*w&s*-

Artist Who Happens to Be a Chimp Sells 40 Finger Paintings. (*James E. Darby*)

-*w&s*-

Educationizing of Army a Failure Englishwise. (*Oliver Howard*)

-*w&s*-

Modern Museum Is Startled by əssᴉʇɐW Picture. (*Betsy Wade*)

-*w&s*-

And take your pick of these two, written on opposite sides of the Atlantic for the same story: "London Theatre Named for—er—Prince Charles" (*Robert Shelton*, New York), "Top British Actress Fluffs a Royal Line" (*William Mahoney*, International Edition).

HEADQUARTERS. *See* "whereabouts."

HOPEFULLY. "Hopefully, two-thirds of this cost would be covered by Federal grants." This solecistic use of "hopefully" probably arises from a false analogy. You can use adverbs like "fortunately" or "luckily" in this way. They mean "in a fortunate [or lucky] manner," and in the kind of construction cited would be equivalent to "it is fortunate [or lucky] that." But "hopefully," as used here, does not mean in a hopeful manner, nor is it equivalent to "it is a hopeful thing that." The intended meaning is "it is hoped that" or "if hopes are realized." Phrases such as those would have to be used in place of the adverb.

HOUSEWARES. "Houseware Show Hailed as Success." Believe it or not, there's no such word as "houseware"; it's "housewares."

HYPHENS. Hyphens can cause troubles entirely disproportionate to their size. The catalogue of such troubles is endless, but only three will be discussed here.

1. Hyphens are properly used to join words in a compound adjective, as in "a 54-to-28 Senate vote" or "a coast-to-coast tour." But when these same words appear in independent phrases (usually adverbial) hyphens are improper. These, then, are wrong: "Dividing closely on party lines, the Senate voted, 54-to-28, to table. . . ." "Truman Will Stump Coast-to-Coast."

2. A more esoteric principle is involved in the use of the suspensive hyphen, as in the phrase, "pre- and postsatellite," where the hyphen shows that the first element is to be linked to the later one. But that does not permit a sentence such as, "The measure was killed in a well-timed and executed maneuver." In the phrase "well-timed and executed," we have what might be called a locked-in hyphen; there is no positive way of indicating that its force is to carry over to the later word. The solution is to repeat the element that has been omitted. Make it, "well-timed and well-executed maneuver."

3. Sometimes a hyphen means a period, in a manner of speaking: "Premier Castro read a Cuban naval report citing nine specific instances of United States Navy craft having been sighted operating near the Cuban coast between May 6-11." The hyphen unites the two dates into a period of time, making the "between" inappropriate. You could write, "in the period May 6-11," or, "between May 6 and 11," or "from May 6 to 11," but not "between May 6-11."

HYPOTHECATED. "Expert judgment had established that a nuclear war of the hypothecated proportions would not extinguish all human and animal life." "Hypothecated" means deposited as security for a loan. The word desired here is "hypothesized," meaning assumed or taken as a hypothesis.

IDENTIFICATION. "Tallulah Bankhead, an actress, was slightly injured last night in a fall." Oh, you mean *that* Tallulah! The "an" is, of course, absurd. You have three possible wordings in providing identifications of this kind and the one you select will depend on your judgment of the person's prominence. At one extreme is the person known to almost everyone who reads (and Tallu qualifies here); such a person would rate "the." At the other extreme is the person known only to her mother and the other girls in the show; such a person would rate a humble "a" or "an" (Minnie Glutz, an actress). If the person falls between these extremes or you are undecided about her status, you will usually be safe in using no article (Mary Fickett, actress).

IN ANOTHER DEVELOPMENT. *See* "meanwhile."

IN CONNECTION WITH. The phrase "in connection with" is a soft, all-purpose compound preposition. To many writers it has an impressive sound that, they feel sure, will divert attention from their failure or inability to choose a more precise preposition. Examples of its misuse can be amassed, but one will suffice. "There was a certain amount of good-natured needling between the Governor and the Mayor in connection with the respective contributions of state and city to solving the city's problems." All the writer meant here was "about." Of course, the phrase has its legitimate occasions. For example, a story spoke of an American proposal concerning underground atomic explosions and continued: "This proposal was made in connection with the United States plan for a phased approach to an atomic test ban. . . ." The two proposals were actually linked; they were connected. Therefore, "in connection with" was proper. Watch out, too, for "in this connection." That one can usually be amputated and no one will feel any pain.

INSERTS AND BRACKETS. In inserting bracketed matter into a story the editor should make certain that the relevance of the bracketed matter is instantly apparent. What happens occasionally is something like this: The story relates that the President, in receiving the Ambassador of Slobemia, voiced hope for Slobemia's prosperity. Comes then a bracketed paragraph saying that Congress has passed a bill requiring that bladgets be affixed to every portisframe in the United States. Now, unless you happen to know that Slobemia is the world's sole producer of bladgets (and how many of us do?), the connection is not apparent. A recent example shows how a connection between stories can be skillfully established. The Page One story was about an offer of military assistance to Panama by the Organization of American States. The bracketed paragraph was about an economic meeting of the organization in Buenos Aires and it began, "Economic affairs also occupied the American nations. . . ." The goal, of course, is to integrate the bracket with the story and, above all, to keep the reader from muttering, "Now, what the hell is that doing in there?"

IN TERMS OF. The phrase "in terms of" peppers much present-day writing, probably because it has a fine, learned sound. But usually it is all sound, signifying nothing. Example: "He could not have been thinking in terms of the job he eventually was to take." What is meant here is "about the job." Another example: "Since Lee guarantees its fabrics for a 'lifetime,' this cost factor may prove thrifty when measured in terms of decades rather than years." Why not "measured by decades"? "In terms of" usually signifies a translation from one kind of language to another. On this ground the second example can perhaps be defended. But an additional consideration is terseness. The question that must be asked is, Are these words necessary or are they merely a foggy phrase?

INTO. "He dived in the river and swam in the direction of the woman. . . ." If he dived in the river he was already in the water before he performed the action; "in" denotes merely position. The required word here is "into," which denotes direction.

INVERSE RATIO. *See* "mathematical expressions."

INVITING LEADS. Time was when the opening, or lead, of a news story was a matter-of-fact recital of the who, what, where, when and why or how of the news. Nowadays, although the reporter is expected to include all that information in the first two or three paragraphs, we do not insist that it appear in the very first sentence. What we seek, rather, is a lead that arrests the reader's attention and distills the meaning of the story's essential news. The five-W's lead, though inescapable on some routine news stories, often does little to lure the reader on. The inviting lead, on the other hand, beckons him into the story and makes his newspaper reading swifter and more enjoyable. The following leads (with the author's name parenthesized in each instance) demonstrate how quick interest can be aroused:

In the days when ships were wooden and the men were iron, a Navy man carried his gear in a sea bag. Nowadays he straps his sports car down on the flight deck of an aircraft carrier. (*Oscar Godbout*)

-w&s-

Former President Harry S. Truman walked nearly a mile here yesterday at a two-question-a-minute pace. (*Peter Flint*)

-w&s-

American DDT spray killed the cats that ate the rats that devoured the crops that were the main props against Communist agitation in the central lowlands. The result: the hungry, embittered rural population is tending to support the Communist insurgents. (*Homer Bigart*)

-w&s-

That other feller which won more pennants than anybody else for the Yankees before they counted up his birthdays found that even though it was October and he was born in July and had lost the 1960 world series and didn't need the money anyway is coming back to town next season as manager of the New York Mets and you could look it up. (*Robert Teague*)

-w&s-

If a man made $7,000 a year and owed about $29,000, of which $5,000 was payable on demand and $7,500 more within a year, he would know what it's like to be Uncle Sam. The difference is seven zeros at the end of the dollar sign. (*Paul Heffernan*)

-*w&s*-

A 23-year-old probationary patrolman wondered yesterday where the 23,482 other members of the city's police force were. In a four-hour period he put an end to a restaurant brawl, disarmed a gunman on a Harlem street and rescued thirteen persons from a gas-filled tenement. Then he went to the hospital to be treated for exhaustion. (*George Barrett*)

-*w&s*-

If the Paris look catches on in New York, full-grown women will be getting into the movies for half price. (*Nan Robertson*)

-*w&s*-

Bertha 2d, the only live whale to be exhibited here since 1897, is dead because, like many females, she deceived men about her age. (*Murray Schumach*)

-*w&s*-

Well, by gosh and by jeez, that sure is a mighty slick production of "Tobacco Road" they brung down to the old Cricket Theatre for a revival last night. (*Arthur Gelb*)

-*w&s*-

As the new Douglas DC-8 jet slipped through the overcast above Long Island, the project engineer explained the problem of bald men in aisle seats. (*Richard Witkin*)

-w&s-

The Music Grove in Prospect Park usually reverberates to the Sousa sounds of the Goldman band, but yesterday it echoed to Shakespeare and competed with picnickers who preferred to sleep, perchance to dream. (*Gay Talese*)

-w&s-

About inviting leads—here's a story with a moral. Nat Gerstenzang's phone rang on the foreign desk. It was Homer Bigart calling from Pittsburgh, where he was covering Mr. K's visit. "What's the news?" asked Nat, assistant foreign news editor. "Well, Pittsburgh liked Khrushchev and Khrushchev liked Pittsburgh—that's about it," said Homer. A little later the lead arrived—a well-written but matter-of-fact description of the city's warm welcome. Nat called Homer back. "How about what you told me on the phone?" he asked. The result was this lead: "Pittsburgh liked Premier Khrushchev and Mr. Khrushchev liked Pittsburgh." This little story is told with the knowledge of the two parties, both of whom were pleased with the result. The moral is twofold. For reporters: Often the direct, conversational way in which you sum up a story for colleagues gives you your lead. For editors: Getting reporters to highlight the story crisply for you and then going back to them to get it written that way will usually pay off.

JEWISH. "Signs in Spanish, English and Jewish boldly proclaim the best of all possible buys." "Jewish" applies to the religion or the people. It is not the name of a language; the language is either Yiddish or Hebrew.

JUSTLY PROUD. *See* "loaded words."

KILT. "The boy, wearing kilts, was given a place of honor near the altar." One boy wears one kilt, two boys wear two kilts. In other words, a kilt is not like pants.

LADY. *See* "titles."

LANGUISHING. "Alfred A. Knopf, the publisher, is not languishing praise on Postmasters General who see only smut in 'Lady Chatterley's Lover.'" If you're going to write by ear, Manny, listen closely: the word you want is "lavishing."

LAUDABLE. *See* "loaded words."

LEERY. "Consequently the State Department and the French and West German Governments have been leery of disengagement." The word is slang. Why not "wary" or "distrustful"?

LESS. *See* "fewer."

LEVEL. "The program is designed for youngsters of the third- or fourth-grade level." In other—and fewer—words, "third- or fourth-grade youngsters."

LIKELY. "Of the new American League clubs, the Los Angeles Angels likely will finish eighth." Idiom requires that when "likely" is used as an adverb it be preceded by "very," "quite" or "most." As an adjective it needs no companion: "The Angels are likely to finish eighth."

LIMERICK. The point of this item is that any old piece of doggerel is not a limerick. A limerick has a precise form. "For the occasion Miss Williams has written the following limerick: 'I'm saying farewell without any tears; / For I'm looking forward to these retirement years, / With time for reading, perhaps writing a book, / Painting some pictures and even learning to cook.' " Miss Williams is just a singsonger. Praise be that her verse is no longer. It's a quatrain, peut-être. But a limerick? Nyet! Our writer could not have been wronger.

LIMOUSINE. "At 11:55 A.M. the President got into a closed limousine." One owned by a rich millionaire? A limousine is, by definition, a closed car.

LOADED WORDS. Some words can be loaded, putting the writer in the position of characterizing or expressing an opinion. One of them is the innocuous-appearing little word "for." Here's an example: "He was criticized for meddling at a time when East-West diplomatic relations hung in the balance." Or: "Continued United States criticisms of the British Government for following a 'soft' approach to the Soviet Union. . . ." In these contexts "for" is equivalent to a "because" phrase, and thus seems to accept as fact what is being criticized. This was not, of course, the intention of either writer. Correcting the fault requires a little circumlocution ("as a meddler" and "asserting that it is following a 'soft' approach"), but the extra words are necessary.

In a comparable and quite common situation it is all right to say a man was indicted "for the murder" of his grandmother because the murder, regardless of who did it, presumably is a fact; but it may be dangerous to say he was indicted "for murdering" his grandmother since the "for murdering" (read "because he murdered") and the grammar of the sentence connect the man with the murdering. This may seem like a fine point, but fine points can draw blood.

-w&s-

"Mayor George Vergara of New Rochelle, N.Y., has designated Wednesday as 'Mary Healy and Peter Lind Hayes Day.' Justly proud of its son and daughter who have made their mark on Broadway. . . ." "Proud" may be excused as a statement of fact, even though it is perhaps not verifiable, but "justly" is pure opinion and has no place in a news story. The two words together sound like nothing so much as *The Hohunkus Harbinger*.

-w&s-

"Ambassador Menshikov answered the guffaws elicited by his stock alibi for Boris Pasternak's condemnation by party-line critics in the Soviet Union with spirited repartee." "Alibi," a colloquial word meaning an excuse that is faintly dishonest—prefixed by "stock," which is obviously meant to suggest an unthinking parroting—is out of place in an impartial news report. Moreover, in this context it is unnecessary; the factual statement about the guffaws amply gets the point across without compromising objectivity.

-w&s-

"Standards of desirability were set up by the Housing Authority in an effort to exclude from the projects families that would be disturbing, destructive or dangerous. Laudable as this is, it has the practical result of excluding a large proportion of welfare clients who might well benefit from better housing." "Laudable" is a word for the editorial page, not the news columns.

LOCATED. "The canyon is located about sixty miles northwest of the McMurdo Sound base." To locate is to find or fix the position of something, usually with the connotation that some agent is doing the finding or fixing. The use of "located" for "situated" is a catachresis. Often, as in the example cited, no word at all is necessary.

MARGINAL. "Marginal" is a fad word. "Corruption in the Government is said to have been marginal here in comparison with other Asian countries." "A marine expert told a House appropriations subcommittee today that the recent East Coast storms would have a marginal effect on prospects for game fishing there." If "marginal" in each instance does not mean small or little, what on earth does it mean?

MATHEMATICAL EXPRESSIONS. Such mathematical expressions as "common denominator" may be useful in writing if they are shortcuts that avoid circumlocution and if they carry the reader directly to the intended meaning. Sometimes, however, less familiar ones like "geometric progression" merely make a learned sound and compel the reader to go back over the ground to try to find his way out. Take this sentence, for example: "There is an inverse ratio between the length of time a plane has been around in regular service and the consternation its mechanical difficulties cause." A reader would not be likely to find that instantly clear. He would reread it and finally say to himself that it means, "The more time a plane has been in regular service the less consternation its mechanical difficulties cause, and vice versa." There, of course, is your answer: not only a clearer sentence, but also a shorter one. Leave most mathematical expressions to the mathematicians; they understand them.

-w&s-

"Several smaller concerns were willing to sell the drugs at prices two or four times lower." "Times" is used to compare the bigger with the smaller. When the smaller is being compared with the bigger, use the fractional forms: "one half," "one quarter." In the same story this passage appeared: ". . . the major companies were willing to slash their prices by some 300 per cent below those offered the druggist." Let's see now: if the price was $10 and it was slashed 100 per cent it would be a giveaway. Then if it was slashed 200 per cent more. . . . My, it makes the head to swim!

-w&s-

"Also, Negroes here die from three to nine times as often as do comparable whites from the effects of high blood pressure." You only live—and die—once. What was meant, of course, was "at a rate three to nine times as great."

MEAN. "Yesterday's mean temperature—the difference between the high and low. . . ." Not so; it is the middle point between the high and low. Better no explanation than a wrong one.

MEANWHILE. News stories often contain unrelated or distantly related developments, so that the introduction of a new subject seems to require a transitional word or phrase. The prime favorites of newspapermen are "meanwhile" and "in another development (or action)." "Meanwhile" is all right if "meanwhile" (during the intervening time or simultaneously) is really meant. But if the story speaks of the commemoration of the Battle of Britain next Sunday and the next paragraph begins, "Meanwhile, a police court magistrate fined Lord Russell," the "meanwhile" has no pertinence. Or if one paragraph is devoted to a trial last spring and the next paragraph begins, "Meanwhile, the court will hear arguments today," the "meanwhile" is meaningless. As to the phrase "in another development," there is nothing really wrong with it except that it is vacuous and half the time is unnecessary. It should always be weighed to determine whether any transition at all is needed and, if one is, whether a better one cannot be devised. Of course, there will always be the reporter who writes, as one did, "Meanwhile, in another development, fourteen community leaders and educators gave Dr. Theobald a vote of confidence." He is the type who drops two tokens into the subway turnstile to be sure he will get through.

MEDIA. "In the debate over toll TV the mathematics peculiar to a mass media have tended to run away with common sense." No matter what Madison Avenue is tending to say these days, the singular is still "medium" and the plural "media."

MEDIATOR. *See* "arbitrator."

METAPHORS. *See* "mixmaster."

METICULOUS. "The cannons appeared to be a high point in the visit for General de Gaulle. He examined them meticulously." "Meticulous" does not mean careful or even very careful. Derived from a Latin root meaning fear, it suggests timorously careful or overcareful.

MINIMIZE. "Minimize" is, but should not be, used in the sense of belittle, depreciate, diminish or reduce. It means reduce to the least possible, i.e., a minimum. In writing of a NATO briefing on Soviet power it is improper to say, "The threat is in no way minimized. . . ." The thought here is "made light of." In the following instance the writer did not understand the word completely: "These burdens must be faced even while city officials seek to minimize them as far as possible." The "as far as possible" is built into "minimize" and thus is redundant.

MINUTIAE. "And how much minutiae was present. . . ." "Minutiae" is plural; therefore: ". . . how many minutiae were present."

MISHAP. Words occasionally have connotations that do not emerge in the dictionary definitions. "Mishap," for example, means an unfortunate accident, yet it does not seem the appropriate word to apply to an airplane crash that killed forty-seven persons. It suggests something much less disastrous—rather a mischance or unlucky incident. Consulting only his pocket dictionary, a foreigner might be tempted to say that fine spring days are scarce, whereas anyone familiar with the nuances of English could tell him that the word he wanted was rare. It is advisable always to heed these nuances. *See also* "quit."

MIXMASTER. A "mixmaster" in *Winners & Sinners* parlance is the writer responsible for crazy mixed-up metaphors. Such as: "Dr. Bucerius has long been the chief maverick of the Christian Democrats, opposing Chancellor Adenauer's leadership and generally tilting at sacred party windmills." That kind of maverick must be a sacred cow.

-w&s-

"The internal strife gnawing at the country has not only mirrored the 'cold war' but brought it to a hot focus from time to time."

-w&s-

"Secretary Mitchell has been a target of unions, management and Congress, but he still calls his shots as he sees them." An umpire who calls them as he sees them could also be a pool player who calls his shots, but he ought to have better sense than to try to do both things at once.

MONEYS. "Mr. Rockefeller said the fund would start with $16,400,000 in new or reappropriated state monies." First, it would be "moneys," not "monies," just as it is "parleys," not "parlies," or "attorneys," not "attornies." Second, as Bergen Evans points out, "moneys" has a pseudo-archaic flavor. *See also* "plurals."

MORE THAN ONE. This phrase, though technically plural, is regarded as singular. Thus, the following sentence is correct: "Mr. Hannah said that more than one charge of discrimination was involved."

MUTUAL. "Their mutual interest in guns has provided an informal means of instructing youngsters. . . ." "Mutual" has the connotation of reciprocal: If Jones respects Smith and Smith respects Jones they have a mutual respect. However, if Jones is interested in guns and Smith is interested in guns they do not have a mutual interest, they have a common interest. ("Mutual friend," though not correct, is accepted because of the Dickens title, the books say.)

NEED OF (FOR). "Dr. Alvin Eurich called yesterday for a replanning of medical education to meet the nation's growing need of physicians." "Need of" opens a chance for ambiguity; it could suggest a need felt by physicians. A clean-cut instance would be this sentence: "The nation's pressing problem is the need of physicians." More physicians? Or less poverty among physicians? If the former is intended, "need for" will nail it down.

NOT SO MUCH . . . BUT. "The advice of the physicians and the President's decision to go to Bermuda as scheduled were not so much an encouraging sign of his father's condition but rather a recognition of the possibility that the elder Kennedy's semi-comatose state might continue." "Not A *but* B" is a correct construction. But when the "not" is converted into "not so much," the construction must be converted into "Not so much A *as* B." Following "as much" or "so much" the correct conjunction is "as."

OBVIATE. "But any chance for such mediation appears to have been obviated Sunday by the attacks of Premier Fidel Castro against what he called 'the cowardly attitude of the Latin American foreign offices.' " "Obviate" means "make unnecessary." What was meant here was "removed" or "eliminated."

OCCUR. *See* "take place."

OFFICER. "Officer Green is in fair condition with possible internal injuries. Officer Steinbach was treated and released." On the New York police force and most others there is no such title as "officer," although there are police officers, i.e., those above the lowest grade. *See also* "plainclothes man."

ONE OF THE. Two examples of a common solecism: "Mr. Trumbo is one of the writers who has been officially barred. . . ." "She also is one of those fortunate artists who gives a listener the impression. . . ." In each instance the verb does not relate back to "one," but to the group plural of which "one" is a part. To see the error clearly, all you need do is turn the sentence around: "Of the writers who *have* been officially barred, Mr. Trumbo is one" or "Of those fortunate artists who *give* a listener the impression . . . she also is one."

ONE OR MORE. "Inside each folder is one or more sheets of heavy printed paper, a mimeographed list of state officials and agencies and a stout manila envelope." Even if the subject of the sentence were not a compound one— that is, if the sentence ended after the word "paper"—the verb still should be plural. Like "one or two," which means a few, "one or more" is considered as an entity; it is a phrase equivalent to "some," hence takes a plural verb. Make it "are."

OTHER. "Florida contains more birds than any state in the Union." Phrased this way, the sentence seems to exclude

Florida from the Union. What is needed is "any *other* state in the Union." However, when a superlative rather than a comparative is used, "other" is not included: "Florida has the most birds of all the states in the Union." *See also* "superlatives."

OUTER SPACE. "Mr. Murray urged immediate resumption of underground and outer space tests." There is no such thing as "inner space." Why, then, the phrase "outer space"? Space is space, or, if you wish to be more precise, it's interplanetary space, interstellar space, etc.

OUTPUT. *See* "agreement in number."

OVERREFINEMENT. When an uncertain writer employs an idiom, he's tempted to dress it up. The result may be something like these:

"Twentieth Century squatters—some sitting prettily —are showing every intention of staying put despite the Federal Government's announced plan to evict them." The idiom is "sitting pretty."

-w&s-

"The 73-year-old father of the President was reported to be resting easily." The idiom is "resting easy."

-w&s-

"Sharply at 8 o'clock this morning, 205 women will nudge their way into the Jade Room of the Waldorf-Astoria Hotel." The idiom calls for "sharp" after "o'clock."

-w&s-

"Mr. Yordan, who also wrote the screen play and thus hasn't a leg on which to stand. . . ." The colloquialism is, "a leg to stand on." To what is this fellow up?

PACKAGE. "Package" is a fad word. That does not mean it should not be used. But, like all fad words, it should not be overused, and when it is used it should be used with discretion. In a story about new Western Union services it caused momentary confusion: "W.A.T.S. provides subscribers with lower package rates for heavy users of long-distance service, based on six long-distance zones similar to those used in parcel post service." The conjunction of "package" and "parcel post" was unfortunate.

PANACEA. ". . . We may see the day when that good old American cure-all, the pill, will be the panacea for mosquito bites." A panacea is a remedy for all ailments, a cure-all; therefore the word cannot be properly applied to a single affliction like mosquito bites.

PEOPLE, PERSONS. The ill effects of using words by rote or by rule emerge rather clearly in the two following sentences: "An alarming set of figures just published by the United States Government seems to cast doubt on the proposition that hunters and fishermen are necessarily persons." "Looking like persons at a crowded apartment cocktail party, the Giants and Indians stood close together." It's a good 5-to-1 bet that in each story the reporter wrote "people," not "persons." And if so, in each instance he was right. "People" should apply to groups or masses, "persons" to exact or small numbers of individuals. In newspaper practice we are most of the time dealing with injuries to seventeen *persons* or a racing crowd of 20,635 *persons,* but that does not mean that a copy editor should grimly resolve that every time he runs across the word "people" he is going to change it to "persons." That way lies itchy-pencilitis. Editing is, among other things, an exercise of judgment, not an I.B.M. process.

PERSONNEL. "Three military personnel and some civilians came with Mr. Long to Galveston." Personnel means the body of soldiers, workers or whatnot; it does not refer to individuals. Therefore, you don't speak of "three personnel."

PERSUADE. *See* "convince."

PLAINCLOTHES MAN. A local constable pleads for making a proper distinction between "plainclothes man" (more properly "plainclothes patrolman") and "detective." The plainclothes man's primary duty is to handle vice, gambling and liquor violations; the detective's job is to investigate crime, including being present in civilian dress at any spot where trouble is expected. A piece about Maria Callas's appearance at the "Met" said, "A contingent of plainclothes men from the Police Department was in the theatre." In accordance with the foregoing definitions these were undoubtedly detectives.

PLURALS. Plurals of proper names ending in "y" are formed by adding "s." Thus you would write, "the two Germanys," not "the two Germanies." There are a few (very few) exceptions to this rule, such as the Two Sicilies, the Rockies and the Alleghenies. But forget the exceptions and remember the rule. *See also* "moneys."

-w&s-

"Pi's were tossed about and practically every known angle was worked at the second annual Suffolk County Math Fair here today," Overrefinement, perhaps? The plurals of Greek letters take no apostrophes. On the other hand, plurals of letters in the English alphabet do take apostrophes. In writing of the American Association of Advertising Agencies it is not correct to refer to it as "the 4 As." Make it "4 A's" or "Four A's."

PLUS. "This, plus a change in top management of the brewing company, are believed to be the factors responsible for the switch in advertising agencies." "Plus" means augmented or increased by; it is not the equivalent of "and." Therefore the subject remains singular: "is." *See also* "as well as."

PODIUM. "President Ayub, wearing a gray summer suit, white shirt and gray necktie, gripped the podium tightly as he answered questions." Toehold? A podium is a platform or dais that you stand on or sit on. Therefore, you don't grip it, as you would a lectern.

POLITICKING. "And with nearly 100 new Federal judgeships dangling in Washington, there are excellent opportunities for a little discreet handshaking and politicing." It's "politicking."

PRECIPITATE, PRECIPITOUS. "It was known to reflect the N.B.C. position that TV was still a widely accepted and enjoyed medium and that precipitous reforms in publicity releases, rather than on the air, were not very meaningful." "Precipitous" and "precipitate" spring from the same root, but usage reserves "precipitous" for physical characteristics ("a precipitous cliff") and "precipitate" for actions ("precipitate reforms" or "a precipitate departure"). Mnemonic hint: Think of the "s" in "precipitous" as standing for "steep" and the "a" in "precipitate" as standing for "abrupt action."

PRESTIGE. *See* "agreement in number."

PROPHESY. "In reviewing gains from the joint American-Canadian hydroelectric generating plant at Massena, N.Y., Mr. Moses prophesied even greater savings for users of current from the Niagara Falls plant now being built." Although "prophesy" is a synonym for "predict," it has the connotation of inspiration or occult knowledge. "Predict" is the better word to denote an inference based on facts. "Prophesy" is a word that should find little place in news writing, but occasionally it is suitable: "This golden age, the Mayor prophesied, would be 'one which will find public and private effort and enthusiasm dovetailing to produce maximum benefits to those who live, work and seek recreation in our city.'" The Mayor was speaking of a vision rather than of a picture based on information.

PROPOSITION. "Even educational television, a noncommercial proposition, shared in the glamour of the presentations." "One-world television is becoming a live proposition." A proposition is a well-delineated proposal. The use of the word to mean an enterprise, affair or project is colloquial.

PROTOTYPE. "The prototype model, which will be shipped to the Los Alamos Scientific Laboratory. . . ." A prototype is a first model of something. Delete "model."

PUBLICIST. "Publicist Found Dead." The man was a press agent. "Publicist" originally referred to an expert on public law and then was more loosely applied to those who wrote on public issues. Despite the dictionary, need we debase the word still further?

PURPORT. "The formal charges do not say whether the alleged overcharges were purported to have been pocketed by Mr. Wholey or passed along to the building agents." Both Fowler and Evans point out that "purport" cannot be used in the passive voice. Bergen Evans puts it this way: " 'Purport' cannot be used in the passive, since its significance is already passive—standing for, 'is supposed, is represented to be.' "

QUESTION MARKS. An unquoted interrogatory sentence contained within another sentence is preceded by a comma, begins with a capital letter and ends with a question mark. For instance, "The question is who is telling the truth" should be, "The question is, Who is telling the truth?" The following is likewise improperly punctuated: "The question was, where did the blood triglycerides come from, the person's own fat tissues or the normal conversion of carbohydrate to triglycerides that remained in the blood." The word "where" should be capitalized and the sentence should end with a question mark. An exception would be a sentence containing an interrogation in the form of an indirect question: "The question was where the blood triglycerides came from, etc." In that event there would be no comma, no cap, no question mark, no nothing.

QUIT. Some words have overtones that the dictionary definition does not quite catch. The word "quit," for instance, often suggests a renunciation, even a huffy one. Therefore, when a professor is retiring, the headline "Historian to Quit Yale Post in June," though technically correct, is not altogether satisfactory. *See also* "mishap."

QUIZ. "Eichmann Calm as Quizzing Ends." "Quiz" denotes an informal questioning to test a person's knowledge. It is best restricted to the campus and the TV screen. Certainly it should not be applied to anything as formal and solemn as a cross-examination in court.

QUOTATIONS. Peril is entailed in editing copy so that a person is quoted as having made a statement he did not make. For example, as printed a story said: "Mr. Levinson noted that in recent years the West Side area had seen an influx of migrants from Puerto Rico." Actually, Mr. Levinson had been very careful not to say this. The story as originally written read: "Mr. Levinson termed the change in the West Side neighborhood a 'touchy situation.' In recent years the area has seen an influx of migrants from Puerto Rico." This is an instance in which the editor's commendable desire to cut extra words led him astray. Such editing can well embarrass the person quoted, can harm the reporter in his future contacts and can create distrust in the newspaper itself.

-w&s-

Direct quotations are often preferable to paraphrase. They add color, immediacy and a human touch. If the politician says, "I wouldn't take the nomination if it was offered to me by Brigitte Bardot wearing a bikini," don't write, "He indicated he would not accept the nomination."

-w&s-

In picking up a fragment of a quotation the writer is in charge of his own part of the sentence at least and can frame it to avoid a faulty locution. Why, then, should we encounter a wrong ellipsis such as this: "We have in the past and will continue 'to gather by every possible means the information required to protect the United States' "? Why not, "It has been our practice and will continue to be our practice 'to gather, etc.' "? And here is a sentence that almost goes out of its way to split an infinitive: "Another resolution appealed to the United Nations to 'ceaselessly pursue its goal to keep the Suez Canal open.' " If "appealed to" were changed to "urged that," and the second "to" were dropped, all would be well. As in so many other matters of writing and editing, all that is needed is an extra moment of thought, an extra ounce of care.

QUOTED. News agencies in particular have a curious fondness for the locution illustrated by the following sentences: " 'I'm sorry but we don't serve colored here,' they quoted her"; " 'There's absolutely no truth in it,' the paper quoted Mr. Paar"; "Nothing, the general was quoted." There is little more justification for this bobtail construction than there would be for "the general was reported" or "the general was described." The clause cries out for completion: "the general was quoted as saying" or, to make the tense sequence more precise, "as having said." Sometimes the saving of a few words produces un-English. *See also* "cite."

REBUFF. This word should be handled with care. It means not merely to reject or refuse, but to do so curtly, brusquely or slightingly. For example, there is some question whether the attitude of the steel industry was correctly described in the story headed, "Steel Shut-down Begun by Mills; Union Rebuffed." *See also* "loaded words."

RECITALIZE. "In addition to mere recitalizing in the usual way, Mr. Bress is exceptionally fond of audio-visual equipment." "Recitalizing"? No such word yet finalized.

RECLAMATION. *See* "conservation."

REFORM, REFORMED. A branch of Protestantism that is distinguished from Lutheranism is designated "Reformed";

it is erroneous to speak of the "Dutch Reform Church in the Netherlands" or the "Carmel Reform Church in Rock Valley, Iowa." "Reform Judaism" is correct and something else again.

REGISTERED: "Today he is a registered Democrat. . . ." Daniel P. Moynihan of Syracuse University, who knows his politics, points out that you speak of a "registered voter," but an "enrolled Democrat."

REITERATE. "Dr. Brode reiterated the suggestion he made last December that a commission be formed." "Iterate," which is not in general use, means to say or do a second time or often; "reiterate" means, therefore, to say or do over and over again. "Repeat" or "restate" is the better word for a first echo.

RELATION. Although the dictionary indicates that a kinsman may be either a "relation" or a "relative," there are those of us who favor "relative" as being less bucolic. If, in defiance of "those of us," your preference runs to "relation," you still cannot use it this way: "Samuel Clark, who is no relation to Dick Clark. . . ." If you wish to keep "relation," you will have to say, "no relation of." If you wish to keep "to," you will have to say, "not related to."

REMIND. "Lincoln White reminded that the Department on Jan. 16 had announced that all United States citizens desiring to travel to Cuba must obtain passports specifically endorsing such travel." Since "remind" means to recall to one's mind, it must be followed by an object that has a mind.

REPULSE. "Some students are repulsed by the thought of of going into debt for an education." To be repulsed is to be beaten or driven back. The desired word is "repelled," which conveys the idea of aversion.

SAVINGS. "It would mean a reduction of about twenty-five motormen and conductors with an annual savings of $150,000." A colloquialism, and an unnecessary one, at that. Drop the "s."

SCULPT. "The memorial was sculpted by Frederick Wellington Ruckstull." The verb "sculpt," a back formation from "sculpture," is described in the dictionary as "humorous." Use "sculptured."

SEPARATE. "His course was in mid-block with the objective the fence separating Broadway between Forty-fourth and Forty-fifth Streets." You separate two or more things; a single thing (like Broadway) is divided.

SERIES. An example of what Fowler calls "bastard enumeration": "A platypus has a flat body covered with short dark hair, stubby tail, webbed feet and weighs about two pounds." And don't forget, it lays eggs, just as some writers do. What this writer meant to say—and the editor should have helped him to say—was: "A platypus has a flat body covered with short dark hair, a stubby tail and webbed feet, and it weighs about two pounds."

SEVERAL. "Several hundred people soon will be approached on the question of staggering their working hours. The responses, which will be sought from 1,400 to 1,800 of those employed in Manhattan's central business district. . . ." "Several" means more than a couple but not a great many. Fourteen hundred is too many hundreds to be called "several."

SHOWED. "Mr. Leavis had showed himself to be. . . ." "Other critics said that the Leavis attack had showed that he. . . ." "Showed" is not incorrect as the participle form, but is most uncommon. Make it "shown."

SIBILANT. "Just before the program began, a sibilant whisper came from the last row: 'Mildred got here.' " Try that on your sibilator.

SIC. "The Automobile Merchants Association of New York and the Brooklyn and Long Island Automobile Dealers Association will open a drive next Friday under the theme 'You Auto Buy—Now!' (sic)." Fowler says that "sic," Latin for so, "amounts to Yes, he did say that, or Yes, I do mean that, in spite of your natural doubts. It should be used only when doubt *is* natural." Surely there could have been no doubts, natural or otherwise, about the auto dealers' slogan. "Sic" should never be used to clobber the reader into seeing the point of a joke.

SIDEWIPE, SIDESWIPE. "The stolen car sideswiped a taxicab. . . ." "Jim Gentile suffered cuts today when his car was sidewiped by a truck trailer. . . ." "Sideswipe" seems to have been originally a railroading term based on the word "swipe," meaning a swinging blow. Although "sidewipe" is an acceptable alternative, "sideswipe" is the commoner form and more readily understandable, and is therefore preferable.

SIR. *See* "titles."

SITUATED. *See* "located."

SO FAR AS. "The bikini was originally called the 'atome' by M. Heim, and the sky was the limit so far as advertising it." "So far as" (or "as far as") may be regarded as equivalent to a preposition when the words mean "to," or denote the extent of an action and are followed by a noun, as in "I will go so far as Times Square, but no farther." However, when the words mean, to quote Fowler, "within what limits a statement is to be applied," they constitute a conjunction and must be followed by a verb. Thus, in the sentence cited it should be, "so far as advertising it was concerned."

STILL AND ALL. "Granted that on occasion the mere presence of TV can impart a theatrical flavor to an event deserving of serious reportorial study, still and all the Fourth Estate cannot altogether ignore the larger issue." "Still and all" is not only dialectal, but wasteful as well. Why not just "still"?

STRAIT. "He is the third man to succeed in sailing from the Straits of Gibraltar to New York alone." It's the Strait of Gibraltar. Most people tend, mystifyingly, to pluralize the name of every passage between two larger bodies of water. (Could it be because we have all been, at one time or another, in Dire Straits?) Yet a check of a dozen of the better known of such passages discloses only one—Florida Straits—that has a pluralized name, and even that one is also known as Florida Strait.

STRAITJACKET. "Mr. Fougner opposed 'those aspects of the proposed law which we believe to be dangerous because they place real estate in a straightjacket.' " A straitjacket is not a jacket that is straight—that is, without curves or angles—but one that is confining, which is the sense of "strait." One dictionary (care to guess which?) sanctions "straightjacket," presumably on the theory that if murder is committed often enough it becomes legal. But let's continue to be straitlaced.

STRAND. A Tokyo dispatch reported that the liner *Caronia* hit a light marker and suffered a small hole and dented plates above the waterline. Both story and head said that the liner was "stranded." "Stranded" is derived from a word meaning "shore," and if a ship is stranded it has run aground—a far more serious accident than the one described here.

SUICIDE. "Dr. William H. McMahon, Norwalk Medical Examiner, said the cause of death was suicide." The cause of death in this case was a rifle shot. Suicide was the nature of the death or the verdict in the case.

SUMMIT. "The United Auto Workers Union confirmed today reports that it had held a summit-level conference with Ford Motor Company officials last week." How did we ever describe conferences before Churchill reached the summit?

SUPERLATIVES. 1. "The worst of the two power failures knocked out four BMT subway lines." 2. "The new cards were presented to Miss Josephine and Miss Margery. Miss Josephine, as the oldest, again received the first library card." Make it "worse" in No. 1 and "older" in No. 2. The use of a superlative when two things are being compared may be common in colloquial language, but it is improper in good writing. In spite of that incongruous but idiomatic phrase, "best foot forward," a careful writer will employ the superlative only when three or more things are being compared and the comparative when two things are being compared. *See also* "other."

SYNONYMOMANIA. This is also called "monologophobia"; it's the overwhelming urge to call a horse successively a nag, a steed, a pony, a gee-gee and a bangtail. The urge might have helped the highly charged story that said: "A homicide charge against a Jersey City woman who had been charged with . . ." and "Magistrate Thomas Fitzpatrick dismissed the charge against Eileen White, who had been charged in the death of. . . ." But most often it produces this kind of annoyance: ". . . Billy Jurges' rampant Red Sox completed the rout of the Yankees by crushing the Bombers in the Series finale." Are the Bombers something different from the Yankees? Why the synonym?

A serviceable guide might be this: A synonym is desirable if it avoids monotony (see the charged story above) or if it provides pertinent additional information or identification. It is completely proper, for example, if the first paragraph of the story mentions Steven Rockefeller, to refer to him in the second paragraph as the 23-year-old son of the New York Governor. But if the first paragraph of a story speaks of an elephant, the use in the second paragraph of "the giant pachyderm" is kid stuff. Never forget that an important part of speech is the pronoun.

-*w&s*-

"Arthritis Linked to Old Cow Germ. Microbe Found in Brooklyn Bovine in 1843 Is Subject of World Forum Here." *Winners & Sinners* hates to pick on that word "bovine," but that's the way it is around here: dog eat canine.

-w&s-

"The fast Army halfback, who rushed the ball from scrimmage for seventy-three yards, took the prolate spheroid from Lewis and fired it to Paul Zmudia." Who called that ellipsoidal pigskin a prolate spheroid?

TAKE PLACE. "The crash took place at about 8 A.M. as the three-car train neared Catanzaro." Although dictionaries define "take place" as meaning come to pass or occur, usage seems to favor confining it to that which is prearranged or scheduled. "Occur" is used for that which is spontaneous or accidental. Therefore a crash does not take place and a commencement does not occur.

TALISMAN. A correspondent who should know criticizes this sentence: "In court yesterday she nervously fingered a St. Christopher's medal, a safety talisman for travelers." His letter points out that a talisman is something that produces extraordinary effects—an amulet or charm. In the Roman Catholic Church, he says, such a medal is not considered to produce any effect, but rather "may be the occasion whereby a person prays to God . . . for some divine assistance such as safety in travel." Which serves to reemphasize the point that in sensitive matters like religion extra care in writing is imperative.

TAPS. ". . . 'Taps' has been sounded and the eulogies have been read." Three things should be noted about the word "taps." Since it is not the name of a musical composition but, like reveille, a military signal: (1) it is not put in quotation marks and (2) it is not capitalized; moreover, (3) it is a plural noun. Therefore: ". . . taps have been sounded."

THINK. *See* "feel."

TILL. "Mrs. Payson did not say so, but one could almost read the 'wait 'til tomorrow' expression on her face." There is a word "until," there is a word "till" and dictionaries show an obsolete word "til" (no apostrophe). But nowhere does the word " 'til" appear, and why should it?

TIME ELEMENT. Two guides should be kept in mind for placement of the time element in the lead of a story: First, it should appear inconspicuously, which means usually (but not always) somewhere after the verb; and second, it should sound natural, not strained. In each of the following leads the virgule (/) indicates where the time element might better have been placed:

The Very Rev. James Albert Pike exchanged today a deanery on Morningside Heights/for a bishopric on Nob Hill.

Premier Pierre Pflimlin won tonight a new endorsement/of his struggle to maintain the parliamentary regime.

An Air National Guard jet trainer today rammed into the side of a Capital Airlines passenger plane/, killing twelve persons.

The Social Democratic party congress adopted today a more militant policy on German reunification/.

Perhaps the best way of determining the natural place for the time element is to read the sentence aloud. (And if a man with a white coat and a net comes after you, tell him you're rehearsing for a play.)

-w&s-

Talking about time, here's another recurring problem: "He joined the *Seawolf* on March 1, 1957, and returned last January after a six-months tour at the nuclear power school here." There are three possible ways of writing about that tour and the way it appears in the sentence quoted is none of them. You can say, (1) "a six-month tour," (2) "a six months' tour" or (3) "a tour of six months."

TIMES. *See* "mathematical expressions."

TITLES. "An American who pretended to be a British peer and who was wanted for forgery was arrested yesterday by the Federal Bureau of Investigation. The suspect, who had masqueraded as a Sir Douglas Bedford. . . ." A "Sir" is not a peer. A peer is a baron, a viscount, an earl, a marquess or a duke, but not a knight or a baronet, both of whom bear the title "Sir."

-w&s-

In British usage "Dame" is equivalent to "Sir." Therefore to speak of "Dame Pankhurst" is as ridiculous as to speak of "Sir Churchill" or "Sir Raleigh." Neither title is ever coupled with the family name, but only with the full name or the first name alone. Moreover, the wife of a "Sir" (a knight) is "Lady" plus surname. You do not say, "Sir Winston and Mrs. Churchill"; it's "Lady Churchill."

-w&s-

"A festive spirit reigned and His Majesty had a number of 'gifts' to distribute." "Iran's finest athletes and bandsmen performed before His Majesty." No disrespect meant, but it is best to avoid such respectful forms of reference. Except in quoted matter, most newspapers don't use "His Majesty" any more than they refer to an ambassador as "His Excellency" or to the Mayor as "His Honor."

TROVE. "A Pre-Inca Trove Is Found in Peru." Know what a trove is? It's something that's found.

TYPE. On several occasions *Winners & Sinners* has fired rockets at the use of "type" as part of a compound adjective, as in "debate-type radio or television programs" or "Batista-type dictatorship." This does not mean, however, that "type" is per se a ba-ba word. If a reporter writes that a Hollywood producer is "a nattily dressed, gray-haired, executive type," there is no reason for the copy editor to think he is in a frying pan and to jump into the fire of changing it to "executive-looking man." "Executive type" is fine; "executive-looking man" introduces a different solecism. "Looking" combines to make an adjective, all right, but it combines with another adjective —as in "good-looking" or "odd-looking." It almost never combines with a noun, which "executive" is in this context. Of twenty-four examples given in Webster II, all but one combine an adjective with "-looking"; the one exception is "sailor-looking," and Heaven only knows where they dug that one up.

UNTIL. *See* "till."

VARIETY. *See* "agreement in number."

VERDANT. "Colorful against the park background of verdant greenery were the young girl dancers." Verdant is the color of greenery.

VERDICT. The School of Law will please come to order. One student, reporting on Supreme Court Justice Hof-

stadter's remarks in an accident suit, said he handed down
"a verdict of guilty." To begin with, a judge does not
hand down a verdict; a verdict is a finding by a jury.
Judges render decisions, judgments, rulings, opinions—
almost anything but verdicts. To end with, guilt is found
only in criminal actions, not in civil suits.

VIA. "The severest type of attack would entail simultaneous
accurate, dispersed delivery, via missiles or bombers, of
nuclear weapons." "Via" means by way of (in a geo-
graphical sense), not by means of.

WHAT. "What is left, usually, are the basic formal inven-
tions that movements inspire." The writer first had to
resolve the number of "what." Although there is room for
debate, this may be judged to have been done success-
fully; the "what" may be considered to stand for "that
which" or "the element that." However, it governs not
only the first verb but also the second. When there is a
copulative, or linking, verb (be, become, seem, etc.) the
noun that comes first is regarded as the subject. Therefore, the second verb should also have been "is." *See also*
"agreement in number."

WHEREABOUTS. "Since this desperate gesture, the whereabouts of the Dalai Lama have been unknown." Unlike
"headquarters," which is usually plural, "whereabouts"
is singular. Why? Well, "headquarters" contains a noun

—"quarters"—that is in the plural, but "whereabouts" does not; it is an amalgamation of an adverb and a preposition with an adverbial "s" tacked on.

WHETHER. *See* "as to."

WHILE. "Mr. De Sapio is the leader of Tammany and Democratic national committeeman, while Mr. Prendergast is the Democratic State Chairman." "While" is a subordinating, not a coordinating, conjunction. It is properly used to mean "during the time that"; it is acceptable, though less universally sanctioned, in the meanings of "although" or "but." However, in the meaning of "and" it is not sanctioned, and is even branded "journalese" by non-journalistic critics.

Z-Z-Z. That's the sound made by a sleepy-time editor enjoying a good doze with a reporter or by himself. Here are some of the results of such naps:

Caution, winding road. "The important thing about Mr. Bryan's plane is that he can fold up the wings and roll down the highway."

-w&s-

Two-faced head. "Youth of 80 Lands at Rally in India."

-w&s-

Let 'em live dangerously. "Drive Opening Today on Pedestrian Safety."

-w&s-

Well, it seems there once was an Englishman . . . "A musuem official said that a few days ago Mrs. Roosevelt had heard a comment good-naturedly associated with the collection: 'Churchill paints good like Eisenhower should.' " What is this—the *London* Times? The gag, of course, goes, "Winston paints good, etc."

-w&s-

Eh? "Everyone knows that policemen have many talents, but even they probably didn't realize how many until today."

-w&s-

Feet-loose and fancies-free. "The 6-feet-1-inch Archbishop was born in Milwaukee." Edited, obviously, by a 35-years-old copyreader.

-w&s-

Man, that's news! "The job of selecting the jury was carried on in a courtroom that literally bulged."

-w&s-

Spoon feeding. "Now throw in two tablespoons full of chopped parsley and cook ten more minutes. The quail ought to be tender by then." Never mind the quail; how are we ever going to get those spoons tender? (Make it "table-spoonfuls.")

-w&s-

Fast track. The story said that an 80-year-old man, blown seventy-five feet into the air by an explosion, had been only slightly hurt because a workman had run to the spot and broken his fall. Said the story: "The injured man, Edward Gattner, was aided by Gene Ayres, 23 years old, who was working about 100 feet away on Oak Avenue. He said that he saw Mr. Gattner flung into the air. He ran to the back-yard of the home and helped to break his fall by putting out his arms. Mr. Gattner, once an airplane pilot, fell on soft ground." That final sentence may seem to contain an irrelevancy, but let us not be too hasty in condemning it; undoubtedly Mr. Gattner's pilot training, which gave him a certain basic knowledge of aerodynamics, enabled him to take advantage of favorable air currents and maneuver him-self toward the soft ground. Let us turn rather to Mr. Ayres' sensational feat. The *Winners & Sinners* physics adviser, mumbling learnedly about Galileo and Newton, calculates that a body falling from a height of seventy-five feet would reach the ground in about 1.5 seconds. If Mr. Ayres had taken off when Mr. Gattner attained apogee, he would have covered 100 feet in a shade under 1.5 seconds, because he arrived just before the impact. At that rate he could cover 100 yards in 4.5 seconds. Since the world's record for the 100-yard dash is 9.2 seconds, Mr. Ayres clearly is promising Olympic material. Unless, of course, there was something wrong with the story, which is unthinkable.

-w&s-

Eh? "WAF's Visit Ill Boy and Play Their Band." You can play the ponies or play possum or play hooky, but you can't play a band.

-w&s-

Two-faced head. "Sea Desalting Dear."

-w&s-

Nice trick. "Faubus Hints He'd Shut School Before It Opens."

-w&s-

Those starved railroads. "Yesterday morning all trains were met by The Greenbrier's limousines and taken directly to the hotel for breakfast." Nothing but diners, obviously.

-w&s-

Man, that's news! "Engineers to Hear Diesel Talk."

-w&s-

Eh? "Cleric Studies Stars. U.S. Missionary in Rhodesia Uses Self-Made Telescope." How far is this automation business going, anyway?

-w&s-

Eh? "13th Floor Losing Its Absence Here."

-*w&s*-

Epithets. "In the avalanche of praise for these two couturiers, the favorite adjectives were simplicity and elegance." And the best nouns for the writer are careless and thoughtless.

-*w&s*-

Blockhead. "They built their mother-machine out of a wire frame, foam-rubber-padded for softness and terrycloth-wrapped for cuddliness. For human effect, she was given a wooden head."

-*w&s*-

It's how he finishes that counts. "Cleric to Start Fast."

-*w&s*-

Man, that's news! "At the next traffic light, the Latins again spotted their colleague, this time slouched in his seat, motionless, with his chin propped on his elbow."

-*w&s*-

Don't raise the bar; lower the record. "John Uelses complained of being 'cold' and fatigued when he lowered the world pole vault record last week-end."

-*w&s*-

Eh? "If this is true, the results of the week's events will be more favorable to democratic forces inside and outside Ecuador than had been feared."

-w&s-

A landslide. "He has been frequently called on to assist in the board's integration efforts and was the unanimous choice of Dr. John J. Theobald, Superintendent of Schools, for the new position."

-w&s-

Eh? "The possibility that both engineer and fireman had suffered simultaneous heart seizures seemed beyond the realm of the possible."

-w&s-

Yes, but where were the birds themselves? "The society said a second highlight was a great flight of Bohemian waxwings that extended from Saskatchewan as far east as Quebec City, with sprinklings of the birds turning up as far south as New Jersey."

-w&s-

Not from a turnip, but . . . "2 Buildings Give Blood."

-w&s-

It seems to happen to opera singers. "She developed horseness at 4 o'clock Saturday afternoon, but decided to sing in the evening anyway."

-w&s-

Superfluous words. 1. "The lengthy document, which ran to more than 7,000 words, gave details of Mr. Powers' ill-fated flight." Throw out the "lengthy." 2. "A six-pound four-teen-ounce baby girl was born yesterday morning." Throw out the "baby."

-w&s-

Bollixed botany. "The roots of the present Berlin crisis stem from military and political decisions and agreements involved in World War II." Roots don't stem from anything.

-w&s-

Past imperfect. "Originally, the character (Falstaff) was called Sir John Oldcastle, a knight who was in fact Hal's boyhood companion but who was burned as a heretic in 1417. In Elizabeth's time Oldcastle's ancestors were sufficiently influential to compel Shakespeare to change the name." There's nothing like breeding influential ancestors.

-w&s-

Got forsaken. "In the last week, Humphrey himself has been on every TV program except 'I Have a Secret.'" What's the theme music of that show—"I Have Rhythm"?

-w&s-

Bad medicine. "Explaining that he was allergic to hay fever, the guest declined the invitation to ride." Maybe he was also susceptible to being accident-prone.

-w&s-

Eh? "Until recently the Guggenheim Museum was the first Frank Lloyd Wright structure in the city. A prefabricated home designed by the architect and recently erected on Staten Island is the second."

-*w&s*-

The real dirt. "One of the convict leaders said the prisoners were rebelling against what he called poor medical care and filthy sanitation." What is "filthy sanitation"?

-*w&s*-

Relief at last. " 'Sievers will be a great insurance policy for us,' said the White Sox manager, Al Lopez. 'He can spell Ted Kluszewski at first base.' " It's hard to do anywhere.

-*w&s*-

Sky Pilate? " '. . . I don't think the Treasury can wash its hands of this like Pontius Pilot.' " Maybe it should be "Ponti, U.S. pilot."

-*w&s*-

Eh? "Mr. Levitt conceded defeat at 11:35 P.M., less than an hour and a half after the polls closed at 10 o'clock."

-*w&s*-

The broad-minded Mrs. Masters. "Mr. Masters was born in Manhattan and lives in an apartment on West 46th Street with his wife, a boyhood sweetheart and their two daughters, Roberta, 9, and Beth, 6."

-w&s-

'Rong 'rithmetic. "Positive educational values 'even more important than the traditional three R's of reading, 'riting and 'rithmatic' were outlined tonight." And rite speling makes fore.

-w&s-

Man, that's news! "The extract was injected into several mice, which died within two or six minutes. Given smaller doses, the mice recovered."

-w&s-

This kid needs straightening out. "He had become the father of a curly blond-haired boy."

-w&s-

Eh? "Government Securities Register Broad but Narrow Advances."

-w&s-

Eh? "An average of forty German youths are enlisted each day. About forty others are rejected, usually on grounds of physical fitness." Only 4F's wanted?

-w&s-

Good trick. "Triple spotting refers to the practice of putting three spot announcements back to back between shows."

-w&s-

Unhappy holiday. "Bolshoi Dancers Plan a Postman's Holiday." The postman always rings twice, but it's the bus-man who takes the holiday.

-w&s-

Quick, Henry, the spot remover! "There, from 10:30 A.M. until 8 or 9 P.M. Miss Preis poured over fabrics and sketches." Or should it be "pawed"?

-w&s-

A Mecca yet. "Although identified mainly with the Yiddish Art Theatre, which he founded in 1918 and which was a Mecca for Jewish theatregoers on New York's Lower East Side. . . ." Proving that a cliche can be explosive in the hands of the unwary.

-w&s-

Eh? "Carrying a bag loaded with dollar bills of varying denominations. . . ."

-w&s-

Do you mean Max Ennett? "If the opening spectacle showed signs at times of following a Max Sennett comedy script, today's performance might have been from one by Ernest Hemingway." It's Mack Sennett, of course.

-*w&s*-

Billow slip. "Smoke bellowed from the windows of the top floor of the three-story brick structure during the blaze." Must have been a roaring fire.

-*w&s*-

Clever footwork. "Mlle. Wolf wears skirts and blouses to the office. Because of her bicycling stint, she peddles to work in flat-heeled shoes." Picking up some small change on the way?

-*w&s*-

Sleepy-time horse. "Yesterday Mr. Anemone, a 35-year-old truck farmer, said that Arab (a horse) seemed perfectly happy behind the plow." Well, why wouldn't he be, with nothing to do?

-*w&s*-

Certainly is a key personage. "One of the key personages is Prince Sigismondo Chigi della Rovere-Albani, Marshal of the Conclave. He is responsible for the key to the outside lock on the only unsealed door leading to the conclave enclosure."

-*w&s*-

Romanesque. " 'Sick' Transit Men Face Home Scrutiny."
Or, as the Latin phrase has it, "Sic transit bogus illnus."

-w&s-

Eh? "They contend that any affirmative word on a new
car—still nine months away from dealers' showrooms, if at
all—would jeopardize current buyer interest."

-w&s-

From President to slum clearer. "Regional Attack on
City Slums Set in Jersey With U. S. Grant."

-w&s-

Baby talk. "He pinch-hitted in the ninth and grounded
out." He should have hitted a homer.

-w&s-

Eh? "College basketball rose to its highest and lowest
performances of the local season at Madison Square Garden
last night."

-w&s-

Eh? "More photographers and reporters than the room
could accommodate were crowded into it."

-w&s-

One-dimensional reporting. "The campaign for the Oct.
3 elections is being fought the width and the breadth of the
city."

-w&s-

Man, that's news! "Truck Hit by Underpass."

-w&s-

Eh? "A glass of water in a paper cup finally helped keep her awake."

-w&s-

Corpus delectable. "At 5 P.M., Mr. Tompkins said, he saw the man with a woman's body." Please, Sam, this is a family newspaper.

Theodore M. Bernstein,

assistant managing editor of The New York Times, has spent his entire newspaper career on the staff of The Times.

Immediately after his graduation from the Columbia University School of Journalism in 1925, he joined the paper as a copy editor. During World War II he headed the foreign news desk, in direct charge of all war news, and in 1952 he was appointed to his present position. In late 1960 Mr. Bernstein went abroad on temporary assignment to serve as founding editor of the International Edition of The Times, a daily published in Paris and distributed throughout Western Europe and the Middle East.

This busy and distinguished editor has also been a teacher; for twenty-five years he was a member of the faculty of Columbia's School of Journalism, holding the rank of associate professor when he retired from teaching in

1950. His first book—Headlines and Dead-lines, *written with Robert E. Garst*—*has been used as a text in almost every journalism school in the nation.*

Mr. Bernstein, born and raised in New York City, was a pupil at P.S. 10 and attended De Witt Clinton High School. He and his wife, Beatrice, now make their home in Greenwich Village near Washington Square. Until 1958, when his Watch Your Language *was published, Mr. Bernstein was occasionally able to spare time for his two hobbies*—*painting and typography.*

His new and major work on usage, The Careful Writer, *is now in preparation.*